crilet dedicatio

to the three women who have shaped the author's life:

- *mother* – **sarala** – friend, philosopher, guide

- *wife* – **geetha** – critic, companion, coach

- *daughter* – **sriya** – wonder, joy, inspiration

crilet sections

context	vignette
about crilet	3
crilet design	10
crileting	24
crilet backpacking	70
crilet epiphany	81
crilet epilogue	83

about crilet

why crilet

- mantra – condense remarkable insights to live proportionately

- extract insights from the multitude of information and experiences, pick the most remarkable and condense them to internalize

- apply the insights to different facets of life and embrace purpose, contentment, peace – every single day

what is crilet

- combine the **art** – of thinking, acting, reflecting differently

- with the **science** – of following a structured and disciplined way of living

- to **design** a life filled with purpose, contentment, peace

how to crilet

- the orchestration of art and science of living is not a genetic trait – it is developed and honed over time through attention, discipline, practice

- to assist, crilet provides a framework and guideline to a way of living along with a backpack of traits, tools, templates to organize thoughts and action

- the goal here is to seek not so much a balanced life, but more a proportionate one where the focus is on harmonious relationships of the parts (facets) that make up the whole (life)

crilet dictionary

- **crilet** – noun – a way of living, also keepsakes from crileting

- **crileting** – verb – act of creating crilet vignettes and keepsakes

- **criletable** – adjective – amenable to crileting

crilet terminology

- condense remarkable insights (**vignettes**) to make new meaning

- design a **proportionate** life – harmonious **life elements** relationships (spiritual, health, family, passion, learning, creativity, wealth, work, social)

- embrace purpose, contentment, peace (**life essentials**) - every single day

crilet vignettes

- 3 related bullet points or a table about a "context" on a slide – to make new meaning

- pithy maxim – intended to internalize through reflection

- title syntax: "context" crilet (about a context); crilet "context" (about crilet)

crilet design

crilet framework

union of 9 life elements:

learning	passion	creativity
(1.4)	(1.3)	(1.5)
health	spirituality	family
(1.1)	(1.0)	(1.2)
work	wealth	social
(1.7)	(1.6)	(1.8)

to embrace the 3 life essentials:

purpose, contentment, peace

crilet framework design

- **arrangement** – left column – left brain stuff; right column – right brain stuff; center column - convergence

- **flow** – all life elements simultaneously diverge from and converge in spirituality

- **proportionality** – attending to all life elements each week and integrating core principles of each life element into as many daily activities as possible

crilet life elements design

focus:

not so much on symmetry and balance

more on harmonious relationships

and impact and influence of each life element
on the 'whole'

crilet life essentials

every single day:

- **purpose** – listen to your inner voice to uncover your calling

- **contentment** – wanting nothing more

- at **peace** with yourself and the world

crilet spirituality element

principles:

- *inquire within – 'who am i?'*

- *have faith in 'grace'*

- *surrender the ego*

in italics – from ramana maharshi's life and teachings

(1.0 spiritual)

crilet health element

principles:

- physical – focus on hygiene, exercise, diet

- emotional – be optimistic, let go, accept and forgive

- intellectual – be curious, create new, inspire others

(1.1 health)

crilet family element

principles:

do not take for granted

devote time

- support, care, contribute

(1.2 family)

crilet passion element

principles:

focus on:

- what brings you joy just in doing

- what comes naturally and is unique to you

- creating value

(1.3 passion)

crilet learning element

principles:

be a lifelong learner

apply learning to real life

• internalize, refine, iterate

(1.4 learning)

crilet creativity element

principles:

- try new things – explore the power of 'what if?'

- failures are better teachers than successes

- enjoy the journey – it is more important than the goal

(1.5 creativity)

crilet wealth element

principles:

- be self sufficient

- desire less

- focus on quality of life

(1.6 wealth)

crilet work element

principles:

focus on:

- bringing out your best

- learning new constantly

- delivering value

(1.7 work)

crilet social element

principles:

support a cause

give more, take less

help others who cannot help you in return

(1.8 social)

crileting

the art of condensing remarkable insights

starter kit

spark your imagination and attention

and make your own vignettes

to guide your life

crileting principles

principle	how to?
analogy/contrast	comparing similarities/differences
metaphor	representing symbolically
reframe	creating a different way of looking at a situation
juxtaposition	placing unrelated things next to each other for contrasting effect
unity/diversity	seeing unity in diverse subjects
vuja de	déjà vu – new things reminding of old vuja de – looking at old things in new ways
abstraction	extracting the essence
pattern	seeing commonalities and relationships
zoom in/out	freely traversing the big picture and details

crilet analogy

world	world of crilet
natural elements (5) –	**life elements (9) –**
earth, water, fire, air, space	spiritual, health, family, passion, learning, creativity, wealth, work, social
basic needs (3) –	**life essentials (3) –**
food, shelter, clothing	purpose, contentment, peace
fundamental particle interactions (4) –	**fundamental crilet interaction (1) –**
electromagnetic, gravitational, strong, weak	spiritual

practice crilet

- mindfulness – live in the moment

- minimalistic living – live with less so you can live more

- intentional living – live to your values and beliefs

(1.0 spiritual)

silence crilet

- most powerful language

- absence of thoughts

- eternal witness

(1.0 spiritual)

mindset crilet

naivete is essential

ego distracts

humility is grace

(1.0 spiritual)

crilet
live
proportionately

frugal crilet

be frugal with:

- food

- speech

- thoughts

(1.0 spiritual)

diet crilet

right food – proteins, carbohydrates, fats

right quantity – less is more

right time – same time every time

(1.1 health)

growing up crilet

- grow into wisdom

- grow out of materialism

- grow up gracefully

(1.2 family)

parents crilet

to your children:

- give them your time more than money

- be their best friend forever

- teach them the art of time management

(1.2 family)

spouse crilet

to each other:

- be patient, compromise, sacrifice

- be the best critic and supporter

- learn and grow together

(1.2 family)

children crilet

to your parents:

share all thoughts and emotions

• don't overlook their wisdom

lend a ear and care for them as they grow older

(1.2 family)

dreams crilet

- best dreams – when you are sick of the status quo

- great dreams – first jotted on note pads

- practical dreams – when you are awake!

(1.3 passion)

the 3 'i' crilet

imagine – fresh possibilities

inspire – new meaning

innovate – for positive change

(1.3 passion)

imagine crilet

- dare to dream

- build those castles in the air!

- experience the power of 'what if?'

(1.3 passion)

crilet
live
proportionately

inspire crilet

- be the message

- overcome the odds

- make a dent

(1.3 passion)

innovate crilet

- identify – the problem you are most passionate about solving

- ideate – design, build, test your idea to solve the problem

- implement – put to use for positive change

(1.3 passion)

believe crilet

from	to also
in yourself	in your dreams
in your work	in serendipity
in possibilities	in miracles

(1.3 passion)

crilet
live
proportionately

mantra crilet

- defines you in 3 words or less

- exemplifies your work

- chant it daily!

(1.3 passion)

knowledge crilet

general - archaic

specialized – passé

varied – now!

(1.4 learning)

learning crilet

- learning new – what and how to do

- learning from mistakes – what and how not to do

- unlearning – changing what and how to do, based on new information

(1.4 learning)

'how to learn' crilet

- add context to content

- abstract and reuse

- focus on becoming wise, not just knowledgeable

(1.4 learning)

grammar crilet

learn to use social media grammar effectively:

- hashtags

- combined words

- acronyms

(1.4 learning)

think crilet

passé	relevant
value addition	value creation
deja vu	vuja de
order	juxtaposition

(1.5 creativity)

ask crilet

good	better
can i?	can't i?
why?	why not?
how?	how else?

(1.5 creativity)

idea crilet

measures:

mark – ability to freeze you in your tracks

power – application in real life

depth – potential for reuse in varied contexts

(1.5 creativity)

crilet
live
proportionately

write crilet

- condense sensations

- design vignettes

- create stickiness

(1.5 creativity)

adventure crilet

real	virtual
go outdoors	surf the net
body sports	use the right brain
mementos	bookmarks

(1.5 creativity)

design crilet

focus on:

- simplicity

- clarity

- elegance

(1.5 creativity)

seek crilet

not material things

instead seek rich experiences

and association with the wise

(1.6 wealth)

speak crilet

- comment insightfully

- tell a story

- deliver punch

(1.7 work)

manage crilet

expectations

perceptions

diversity

(1.7 work)

crilet
live
proportionately

solve crilet

good	better
for balance	for proportion
for timeliness	for relevance
to fix the issue	to fix the pattern

(1.7 work)

work products crilet

- nail the content

- frame the visual

- apply lipstick

(1.7 work)

crilet
live
proportionately

do crilet

myth	relevant
do unusual things	do usual things unusually
do extraordinary things	do ordinary things extraordinarily
multi-tasking (at the same time)	multi **varied** tasking (at different times)

(1.7 work)

act crilet

now!

step it up a notch... and then some...

• outdo yourself... constantly...

(1.7 work)

crilet
live
proportionately

proact crilet

- check blind spots

- watch leading indicators

- devise dependable alerts

(1.7 work)

crilet
live
proportionately

react crilet

confront the brutal facts

map best tasks to brutal facts

map best resources to best tasks

(1.7 work)

analyze crilet

- remove noise and clutter

- abstract and simplify

- make meaning

(1.7 work)

crilet
live
proportionately

iterate crilet

- do

- refine

- enhance

(1.7 work)

rigor crilet

what is:

- relevant

- optimal

- effective

(1.7 work)

be crilet

be the message

be the change

be you!

(1.8 social)

'tune in' crilet

aha! moments can come from:

- snoopy to umberto eco

- bourgeois to literati

- infant's whimper to grandma's grunt

(1.8 social)

crilet
live
proportionately

attitude crilet

revere the wise

infect with enthusiasm

• attack with candor

(1.8 social)

journey crilet

material	spiritual
an outward journey	an inward journey
external guidance	inner voice
meaning in words	meaning in silence

(1.0 spiritual)

crilet
live
proportionately

crileting template

_____<context>_____

* _____

* _____

* _____

(1.x life element)

create as many vignettes as needed for different contexts or for different dimensions of the same context, to guide your life

crilet backpacking

the science of leading a proportionate life

starter kit

traits

tools

templates

crilet traits

attention – eternal observation

- discipline – to achieve freedom

practice – do, internalize, iterate

crilet tools and templates

- **nia**: notes – ideas – actions tracker

- **gtg**: goals tracking grid

- **atu**: attentive time units (calendar)

crilet nia

notes – ideas – actions tracking:

first – jot down in a scratch pad, before you forget

later – enumerate and group by life elements

over time – convert notes to ideas and ideas to actions

crilet nia template

each line item tracks progress from a note to idea to action

#	life element	note	idea conversion	action conversion
1	1.x life element	description (date)	description (date)	**action #**: 1.x.# description set on: to complete by: **status**: description (date)
2	1.x life element	description (date)	description (date)	**action #**: 1.x.# description set on: to complete by: **status**: description (date)
3	example: (for a class teacher) 1.0 spiritual 1.7 work	read "article abc" to learn more about mindfulness (2/12)	create crilet vignette for the top 3 things to focus in the month of march at work (3/1)	**action #**: 1.1.1 be keenly observant without being judgmental, on body language of my audience in my classes. set on: 2/28 to complete by: 3/31 **status**: list the top 3 things uncovered, to do better (3/8)

crilet gtg

goals tracking:

- 1-3 goals for each life element

- Set them SMART (specific, measurable, achievable, relevant, time bound)

- ensure harmony with other life elements

crilet gtg template

goals tracking grid:

learning	passion	creativity
goal #: 1.4.# description set on: to achieve by: **status**: description (date)	**goal #**: 1.3.# description set on: to achieve by: **status**: description (date)	**goal #**: 1.5.# description set on: to achieve by: **status**: description (date)
health example: **goal #**: 1.1.1 reduce weight by 5 lbs set on: 1/1 to achieve by: 3/31 **status**: reduced 3 lbs (2/21)	spiritual **goal #**: 1.0.# description set on: to achieve by: **status**: description (date)	family **goal #**: 1.2.# description set on: to achieve by: **status**: description (date)
work	wealth	social
goal #: 1.7.# description set on: to achieve by: **status**: description (date)	**goal #**: 1.6.# description set on: to achieve by: **status**: description (date)	**goal #**: 1.8.# description set on: to achieve by: **status**: description (date)

crilet atu

attentive time units (atu):

one 'attentive time unit' – minimum practical duration to plan for productive work without distractions

- 1 atu = 15 minutes; 96 atu = 1 day

- avoid all or nothing syndrome by organizing key daily activities in atu intervals

crilet calendar

organize key activities to align with:

- human circadian rhythm

- interplay of *sattvic* (purity, creativity, peacefulness), *rajasic* (passion, activity, egoism), *tamasic* (dullness, lethargy, inertia) *gunas* (qualities) during the day

- embracing – purpose, contentment, peace

  in italics – sanskrit - from hindu philosophy

crilet calendaring

apporation time to attend to all 9 life elements each week

integrate uplifting life element activities with routine tasks to extract the most from each day - (this is different from traditional multi-tasking which causes distraction by attempting to do multiple important things at the same time)

apply core principles of each life element into as many daily activities as possible - this is the art of bringing the right attitude and mindset to everything we do

crilet calendar template

line items are illustrative examples for a given day

start time	end time	attentive time units (atu)	action	primary life element	integration with other life elements
5:00 AM	6:00 AM	4	5K walk	health	learning (audio book)
9:00 AM	12:00 PM	12	at office	work	
12:00 PM	1:00 PM	4	lunch	work	social (networking)
7:00 PM	8:00 PM	4	dinner	health	family (time with kids)
8:30 PM	8:45 PM	1	read a book	learning	
8:45 PM	9:00 PM	1	create a vignette	passion	

crilet epiphany

crilet epiphany

union:

- combine crilet framework of life elements and life essentials

- with crileting – art of condensing remarkable insights

- and crilet backpacking – science of leading a proportionate life

apply in daily living to lead a proportionate life embracing purpose, contentment, peace every single day!

crilet epilogue

crilet 'about author'

lifelong learner:

- varied career – information technology services in public and private sectors, consulting and trade industries spanning customer support, operations, finance, human resources, recruitment, sales, marketing, engineering, delivery...

- varied personal and work roles – son, husband, father, artist, writer, engineer, consultant, manager, leader...

- varied interests – science, technology, business, music, art, design, theater, religion, philosophy...

crilet conception

author's retrospectives:

1988 – 1996: exposure to western philosophy of objectivism and later introduced to hindu vedantic doctrine - advaita (non-dualism)

- 1997 – 1998: **introduction to ramana maharshi's life and teachings**

- 1999 – 2002: exposure to various eastern spiritual teachings and western philosophies, principles of logic and structure, creative thinking and ideation techniques

crilet birth

author's journey with daughter and crilet!

- 2003 – 2004: to coincide with daughter's birth, author starts working on a model to integrate spiritual teachings of the east with the lifestyle of the west - with the idea that someday his daughter would read and benefit from it – birth of crilet framework idea

- 2013 – 2014: author starts jotting down insights in a 3-point slide format - with the aim of teaching his daughter, life principles in a simple and fun format that is easy to remember – birth of crilet vignettes idea

- 2018 – 2019: as a gift for daughter's 16th birthday! - author combines framework and vignette ideas into a comprehensive model and shares the product with wife and daughter – they love the idea and push author to publish as a book for the benefit of all who may be interested – **crilet is born!**

crilet gratitude

all the world is a classroom and aha! moments have come
from a variety of sources – vedas, realized souls, their
devotees, epics, various other people and their literary works
– the author feels truly humbled and blessed:

tao te ching thirukkural upadesa saram	ramana maharshi ramakrishna - paramahamsa adi shankaracharya	edward tufte dan roam michael michalko
james allen ray kurzweil hugh prather	bhagavad gita ashtavakra gita ribhu gita	a.parthasarathy richard bach erich segal
tom peters steve jobs simon sinek	arthur osborne muruganar nochur venkataraman	robert pirsig guy kawasaki stephen hawking

crilet *pranāma*

to ramana maharshi

the author's -

- beginning

- end

- and everything in between

pranāma – sanskrit – reverential salutation

let's crilet

if these vignettes have set you free to fly, please take a moment to share your view – there's many a sight the author is yet to see...

www.crilet.com

gokulbala@crilet.com

Printed in Great Britain
by Amazon

63576974R00051